Red

Deep blue

THE
PATCHWORK
POCKET PALETTE

A Handy Visual Guide
to Mixing and Matching
Colored Fabrics

ANNE WALKER

CHRONICLE BOOKS
SAN FRANCISCO

First published in the
United States in 1995
by Chronicle Books.
Copyright © 1994
Quarto Inc.

Library of Congress
Cataloging in
Publication Data
available.

ISBN 0-8118-0885-8

Distributed in Canada
by Raincoast Books
112 East Third Avenue
Vancouver, B.C.
V5T 1C8

Published by
Chronicle Books
275 Fifth Street
San Francisco
California 94103

A QUARTO BOOK

This book was designed
and produced by
Quarto Inc.
The Old Brewery
6 Blundell Street
London N7 9BH

10 9 8 7 6 5 4 3 2 1

While every care has
been taken with the
printing of the color
charts, the Publisher
cannot guarantee total
accuracy in every case.

CONTENTS

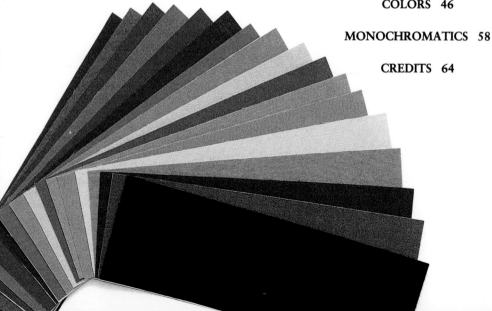

THE COLORS

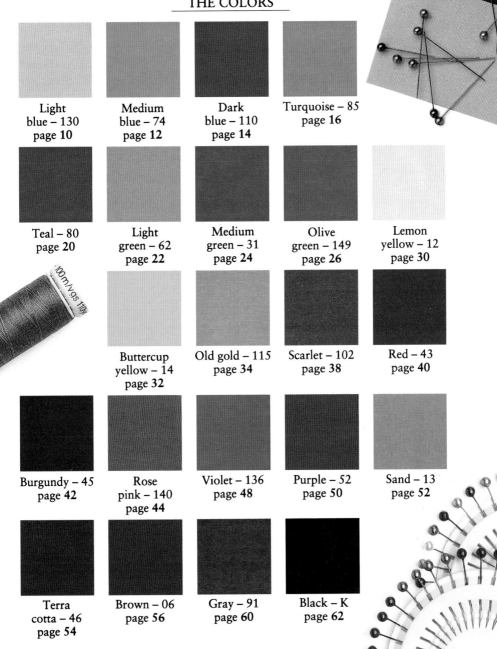

Light
blue – 130
page 10

Medium
blue – 74
page 12

Dark
blue – 110
page 14

Turquoise – 85
page 16

Teal – 80
page 20

Light
green – 62
page 22

Medium
green – 31
page 24

Olive
green – 149
page 26

Lemon
yellow – 12
page 30

Buttercup
yellow – 14
page 32

Old gold – 115
page 34

Scarlet – 102
page 38

Red – 43
page 40

Burgundy – 45
page 42

Rose
pink – 140
page 44

Violet – 136
page 48

Purple – 52
page 50

Sand – 13
page 52

Terra
cotta – 46
page 54

Brown – 06
page 56

Gray – 91
page 60

Black – K
page 62

WHEN YOU PLAN a patchwork project, one of the most difficult tasks is selecting the combination of colors and fabrics to use in your design. The purpose of this book is to provide an easy guide to combining colors for patchwork. Twenty-two principal colors have been chosen from the variety available to today's quilt-maker. Each of these then takes the dominant position in a series of patchwork blocks, and additional fabrics are introduced progressively. Together, these fabric blocks offer almost 400 different color combinations.

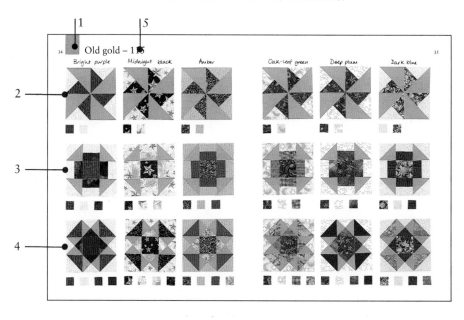

▲ *Each double-page chart features one of the 22 colors, referred to as the "principal" color (1). For a visual guide to these, see page 3. Each principal color acts as the foundation for six different color schemes, and a column of three patchwork blocks is used* *to develop each scheme. The first block of every column combines the principal color with a second color and a background color (2). Subsequent blocks build upon this combination by introducing two further colors (3 and 4). Solid and printed fabrics make* *up the patchwork blocks, and although all the principal colors used here are solid, prints and solids should be regarded as interchangeable. The codes (5) refer to P & B Textiles' solid fabrics, which are used throughout this book.*

THE COLOR CHARTS can be read horizontally and vertically. The columns demonstrate how to build up and integrate colors successfully, while the rows allow you to compare the outcome of different color choices. Because the patchwork blocks on each chart have the principal color in common, they also suggest ways of combining different blocks. As you become more adventurous, you can select blocks from different charts and examine how they work together.

▶ The first row uses a Pinwheel block. The principal color takes the dominant position (1) and a strong second color is introduced (2). A harmonizing background color completes the effect (3).

▶ Here, the colors are arranged in a Churn Dash block. The third color enhances the existing combination and introduces a new element (4).

▶ The complexity is increased, and five colors are brought together in an appealing and well thought-out Ohio Star block.

Small swatches of fabric are placed below each block to indicate clearly the combination of colors used.

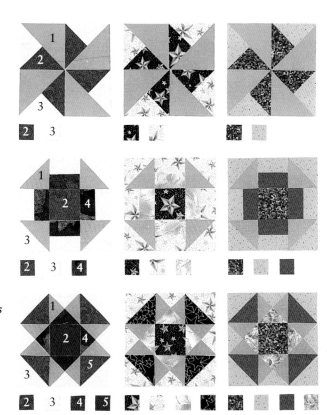

REMEMBER
Each principal color is featured on its own double-page chart. Six color schemes are developed on every chart.

WHEN YOU SELECT the dominant color for a project, your choice may be determined by the room it is to live in, or simply by personal preference. Whatever the reason, this color must then be combined with others in an appealing way. Many quiltmakers feel at a disadvantage at this stage if they have had no formal art training; hence the great demand for color theory workshops. While there is no right or wrong way to put colors together, some knowledge of color theory is useful. Examining how colors relate on a color wheel allows you to predict the way they will work together in your design.

◀ *The center triangle shows the three primary colors – red, yellow, and blue. They are pure and cannot be obtained by mixing. All other colors are made by mixing two of the primary colors in varying proportions. The three triangles which complete the hexagon are the secondary colors and are created by mixing equal quantities of their component primary colors. Tertiary colors are made by mixing a primary with its adjacent secondary.*

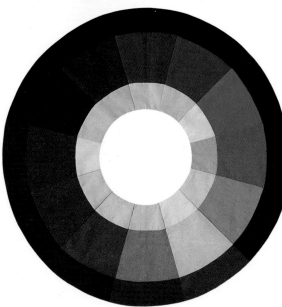

◀ *Here, the color wheel has been split into 12 sections. The central ring shows the hues which lie between the primary and secondary colors. Because the ratio of its component colors can be varied, a color can have an almost limitless number of hues. The colors in the inner ring are lighter than the clear colors in the center; this is because they have been mixed with white, and they are referred to as tints. The outer ring consists of darker colors which have been mixed with black to create "shades."*

It is a good idea to create a personal palette by sorting your fabrics according to color. This exercise can produce some interesting results. It will clearly indicate your own preferences, and you will undoubtedly find gaps in your range. Try to fill these with both prints and solids so that you have a complete palette to select from. Remember, colors do not have to match exactly – experiment using different tonal values, solids, and prints. Mixing colors for patchwork is rather like cooking; you have to "taste" to see if you like it, and by making changes and adaptations, you can create your own visual "recipes."

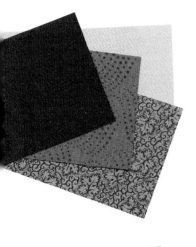

◄ The colors used in your quilt need not harmonize. By choosing those which occupy different sections of the color wheel, you can bring vibrancy and excitement to your work.

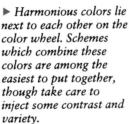

► Harmonious colors lie next to each other on the color wheel. Schemes which combine these colors are among the easiest to put together, though take care to inject some contrast and variety.

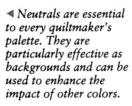

◄ Neutrals are essential to every quiltmaker's palette. They are particularly effective as backgrounds and can be used to enhance the impact of other colors.

► Your personal palette should include fabrics which vary in tone from light to dark. Using a range of different tones will allow you to emphasize patterns and shapes in your designs.

FOR AN ATTRACTIVE piece of work, it is important to convey a sense of visual texture. Tones of a single color can be placed on a scale from light to dark, and their relative position on this scale is known as their tonal value. Fabrics with colors of equal value combine to produce a flat, one-dimensional effect. However, by using a variety of darks and lights, you can introduce contrasts and pick out shapes and forms within a design. Because light colors tend to come forward and dark ones recede, the careful use of different values also adds depth and movement to your work. Similar effects can be achieved by combining solid fabrics with prints, which soften the impact of solid color.

◀ *When patchwork blocks are joined together, the placement of color within each block determines the visual impact of the whole quilt. In the block above, the red triangles which form the star are very strong in comparison with the softer blue pieces. If a number of these blocks are put together, as shown, a strong vertical and horizontal pattern emerges.*

▶ *Here, the same block design has been used, but the effect is very different. The light blue fabric which makes up the star has a much weaker tonal value than the adjacent greens, and a cross emerges as the dominant shape. When four blocks are combined, diagonal lines form the strongest element in the design.*

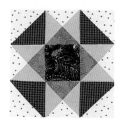

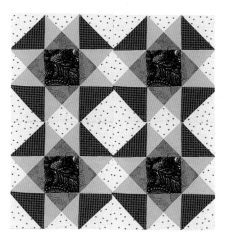

Patchwork made using solid fabrics can look stark. A vast choice of printed fabrics is available, and mixtures of prints, or prints and solids, can be combined to create very different effects. It is important to remember the role of pattern and scale when prints are used – your work should look good both close up and from a distance. Experiment with swatches of fabric until you achieve the look you want.

◀ *Small prints bring a soft, textured feel to patchwork without distracting the eye and can be used to unify areas of solid color.*

▶ *Large-scale prints work well with both solid and patterned fabrics, but care should be taken not to overwhelm a design when using more than one. With judicious cutting, large prints create attractive recurring motifs.*

▼ *Fabrics which have a textured appearance add interest to your work. Like small prints, they offer a softer alternative to solid color.*

▼ *Conversational or novelty prints are fun to work with and great for making items for children. They also add an element of surprise to more formal patchwork.*

▼ *Geometric or directional prints create movement by encouraging the eye to move over the surface of the fabric. They lend themselves to dramatic modern effects and striking contrasts.*

Light blue – 130

Plum   Light yellow   Forest green

Dark pink   Peach   Bright turquoise

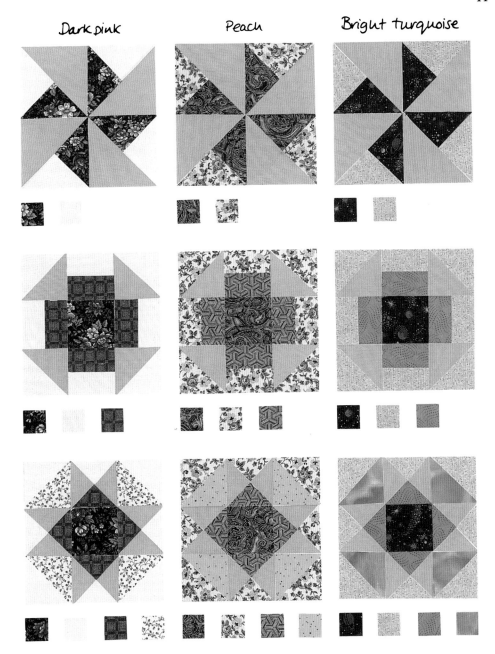

Medium blue – 74

Ruby red   Fern green   Sunflower gold

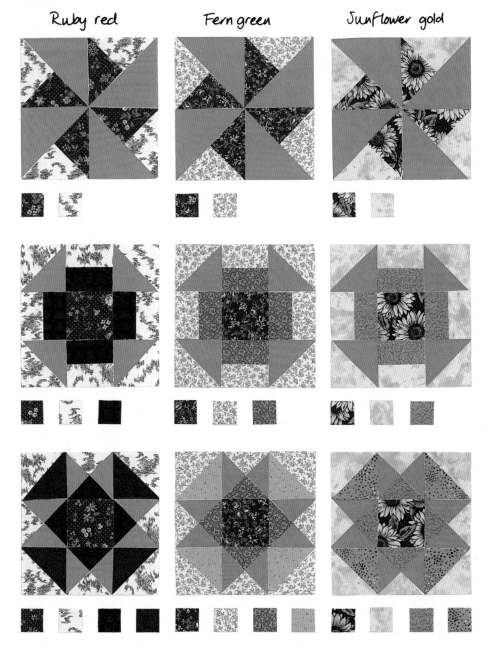

Golden brown   Pastel pink   Jade green

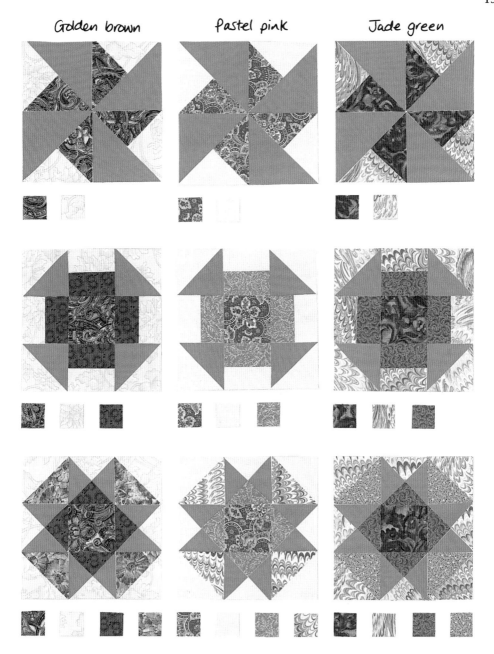

Dark blue – 110

Jade green   Warm yellow   Rich brown

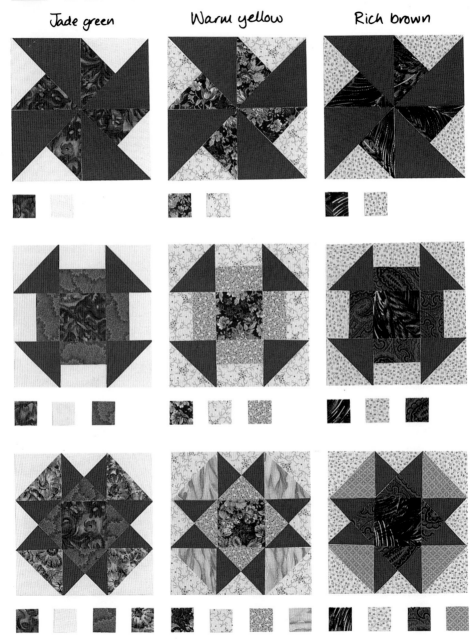

Sugar pink   Sage green   Magenta

Turquoise – 85

Black Imperial purple Deep blush

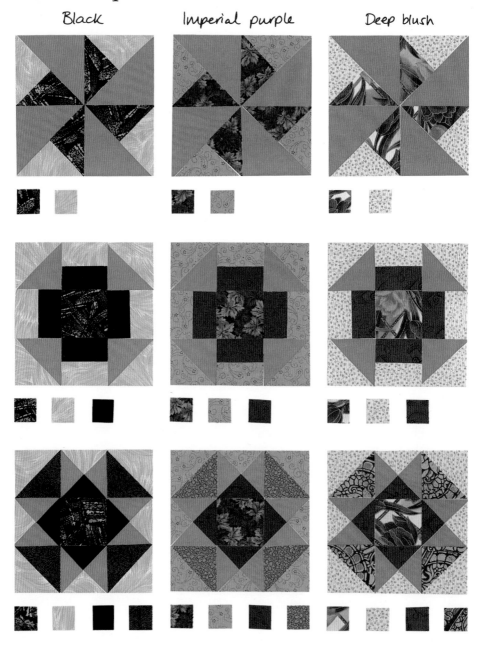

Salmon pink   Butterscotch   Bright red

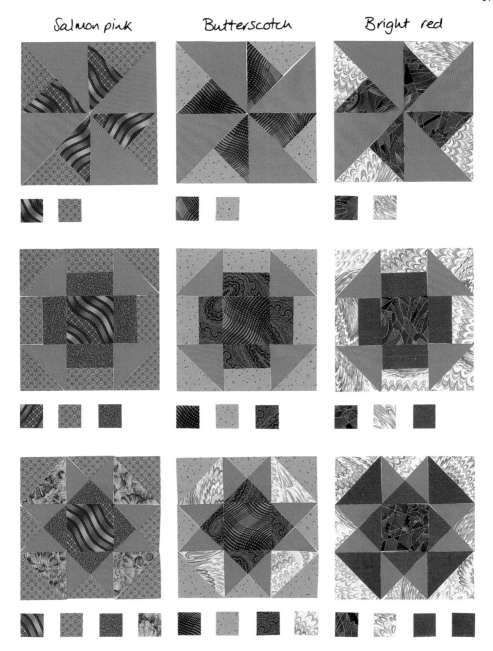

Using Warm and Cool Colors

OUR PHYSIOLOGICAL RESPONSES mean that we accord colors different qualities of warmth and coolness. Warm colors are reds, oranges, and yellows – those associated with heat and light – while the blues, greens, and violets of the spectrum are cool and more subtle in their effect. When they are combined, warm colors come forward and cool colors recede, and dramatic effects can be created when the proportions are changed. For instance, splashes of warm color enliven a cool quilt, while cool accents in a predominantly warm quilt suggest depth and define shape. Since this association between color and temperature exists, quilts can be created to fulfill a particular need – to warm up a cold room or introduce a note of calm in a busy environment.

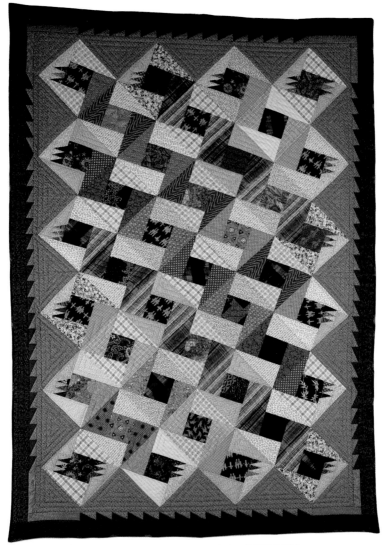

◀ IRENE KAHMANN
"Mikado"
40 x 48 inches
A variety of silks hand-dyed in a range of tints and shades of red give a warm feeling to this quilt. The splashes of cool blue and violet give contrast and definition to its abstract design, and intensify the warmth of the reds.

▲ GILL TURLEY
"Blue Nor'-Easter"
60 x 83 inches
Colors ranging from ice blue to deep indigo are incorporated in this quilt. Its cold look is accentuated by a jagged design with long, thin triangles at the ends of each zigzag. The neutral surround adds no warmth to the effect.

Teal – 80

Sky blue   Mass green   Sugar pink

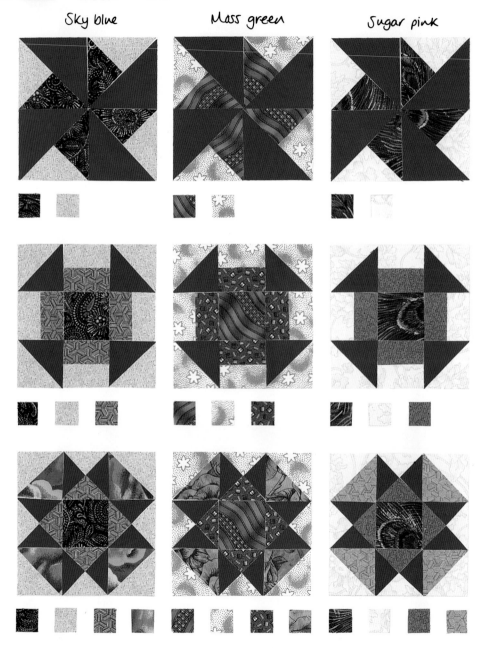

Imperial purple

Beige

Deep rose

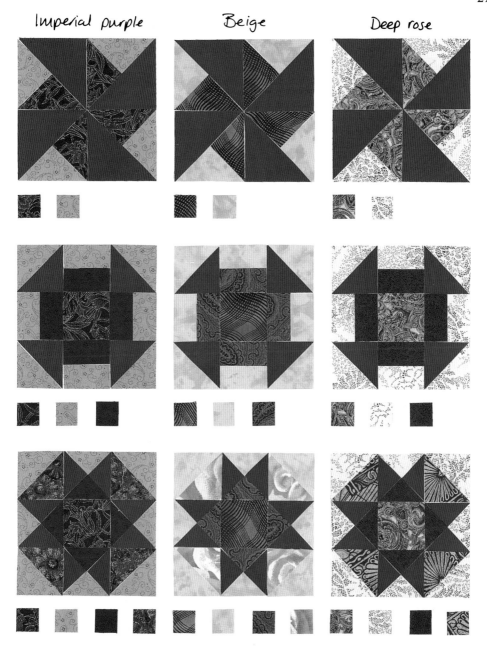

Light green – 62

Beige   Soft blue   Sunflower yellow

Plum   Pastel pink   Lilac

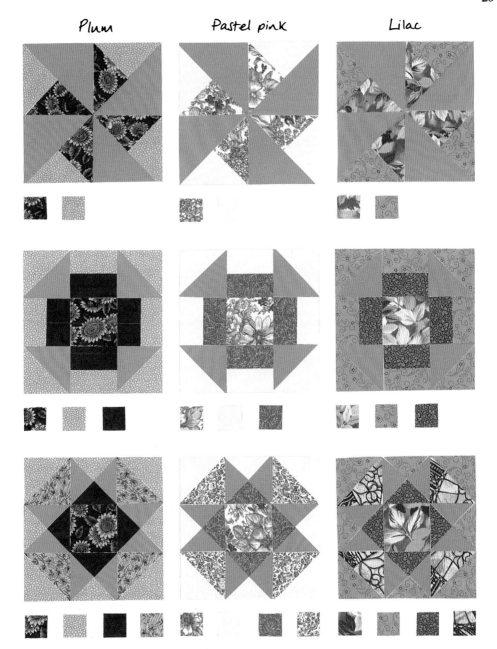

Medium green – 31

Burnished gold   Deep magenta   Sapphire

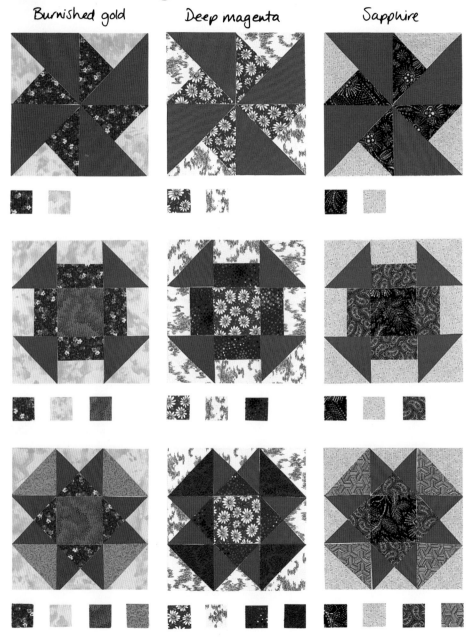

Blush

Imperial purple

Burnished orange

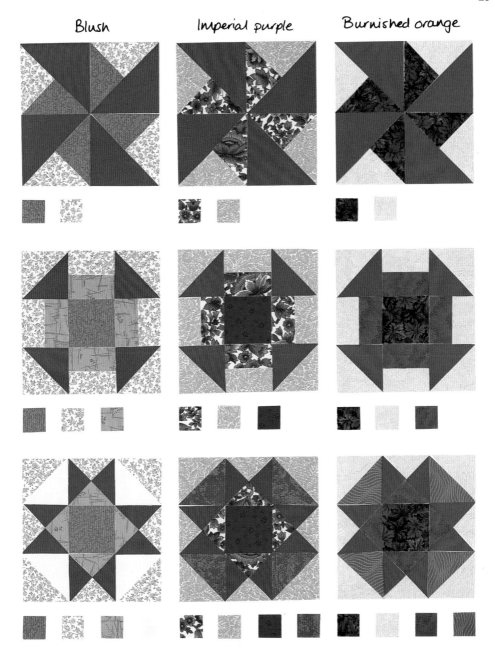

Olive green – 149

Deep red   Periwinkle blue   Burnished orange

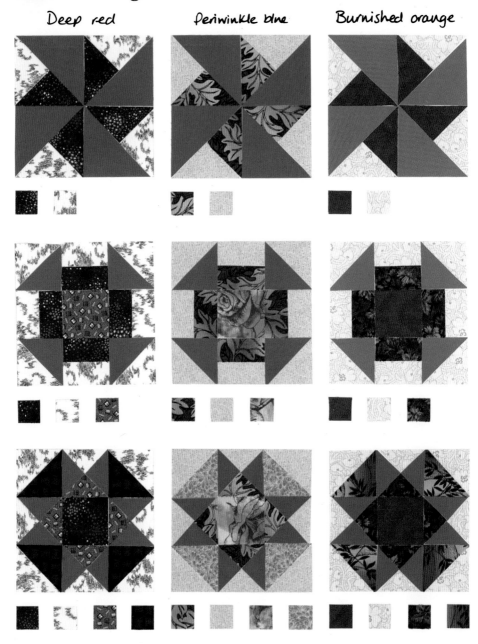

27

Marigold   Imperial purple   Salmon pink

NINETEENTH-CENTURY SCRAP quilts are admired for the stunning effects they achieve incorporating apparently random collections of fabric. In fact, scraps were often purchased specifically for quiltmaking, and an examination of original quilts reveals distinct color preferences. Typically, browns, reds, black, grays, mustards, indigos, and sharp accents of acid green and bubble-gum pink are set against a background of light neutrals. Combining these colors in a new quilt creates a nineteenth-century feel even when modern fabrics and designs are used. Experiment with this technique, taking note of the colors in any quilt you particularly admire.

◄ "Grandmother's Flower Garden"
71 x 87 inches
This scrap quilt made in Maryland during the 1860s combines browns, grays, mustards, golds, greens, and bright sugar pink into hexagonal flowerbeds. The colors of the English chintz used in the outer border have influenced the choice of scraps used for the central design.
Reproduced by permission of the American Museum in Britain, Bath ©.

▲ ROSEMARY RUSSELL
"Old Before My Time"
68 x 96 inches
This modern scrap quilt has all the charm of nineteenth-century examples. A variety of neutrals provide the background for a collection of stars in many colors – brown, red, pink, mauve, black, blue, yellow, and even acid green. The different scales and styles of print used in the quilt bring liveliness and vigor to the design.

Lemon yellow – 12

Fern green   Purple   Mocha

Flame orange   Ultramarine   Medium pink

Buttercup yellow – 14

Imperial purple   Soft green   Maroon

Golden brown

Soft blue

Flame orange

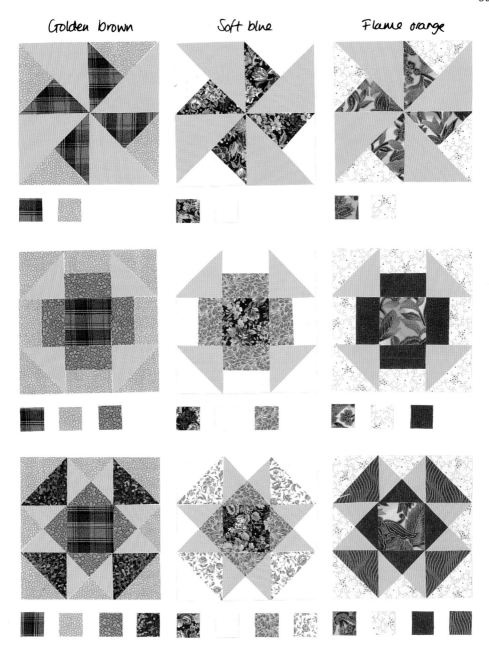

Old gold – 115

Bright purple   Midnight black   Amber

Oak-leaf green   Deep plum   Dark blue

USING BRIGHTS AND PRIMARIES

BRIGHTS AND PRIMARIES create vibrant and appealing quilts. These bold colors work strongly together, and the use of pure hues can produce an almost luminous effect. Their impact can be modified by combining them with either black or white. The combination with black gives a strong contrast, while combining brights with white allows the colors to be seen with their true tonal value. Neutrals also introduce contrasts and help to define shapes and patterns. Because bright colors are popular with fabric designers, there are plenty of exciting prints, solids, and novelty fabrics to choose from: combine two or three colors to achieve a simple, traditional look or, for a more modern feel, use a variety of bright, acid solids and vivid prints.

◄ LOUISE MABBS
"Origami Winds"
30 x 30 inches
Bold rainbow colors are used in conjunction with black. Although strong contrasts exist throughout the quilt, the introduction of a blue inner border softens the overall effect. The use of orange and yellow conjures up memories of children's toy pinwheels on a bright day.

▲ JUDITH GAIT
"Jacob's Ladder"
90 x 95 inches
The combination of solid, bright colors with black and white offers a modern interpretation of a very traditional design. When placed next to the white fabric, the colors retain their true tonal value; this is in distinct contrast to the effect they give when positioned next to the black.

Scarlet – 102

Vivid blue   Marigold   Sage green

Imperial purple   Soft brown   Jade green

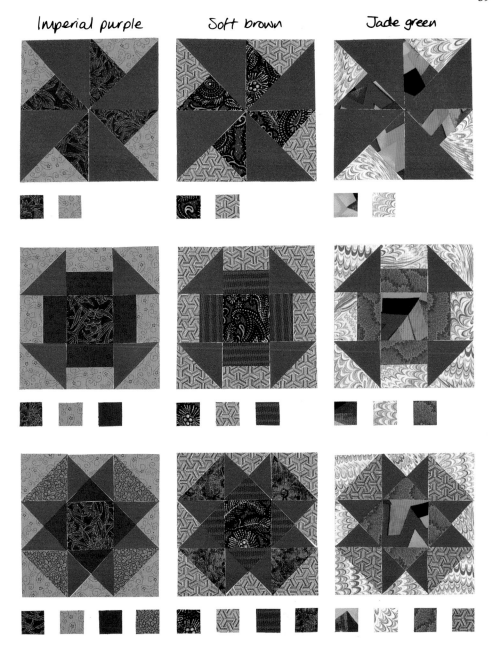

Red – 43

Sunflower gold   Beige   Violet blue

Eggplant　　　　Medium pink　　　　Deep jade green

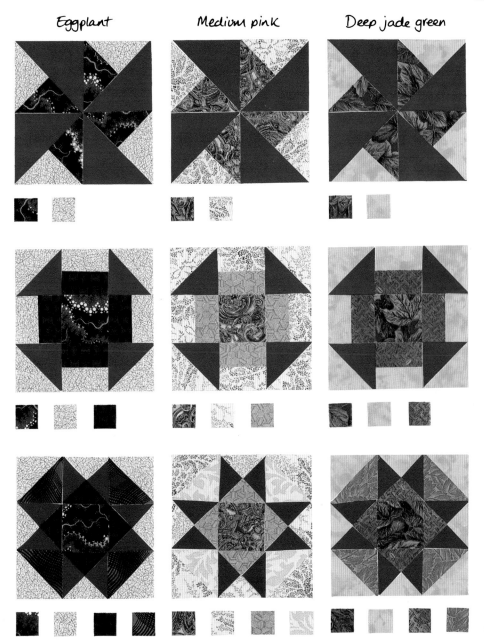

Burgundy – 45

Rich brown   Periwinkle blue   Blush

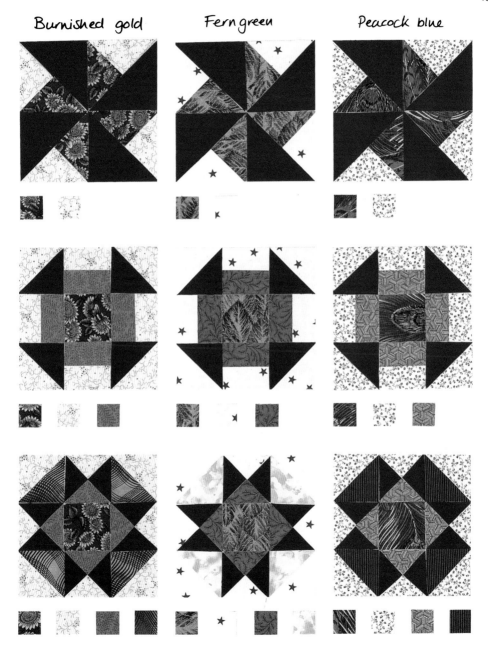

Burnished gold

Fern green

Peacock blue

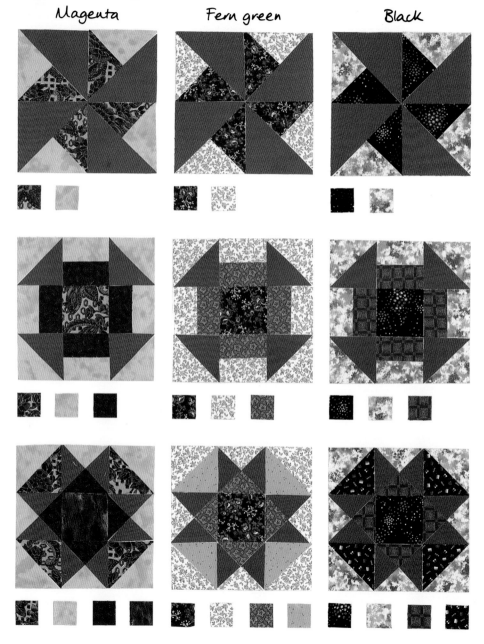

Rose pink – 140

Magenta   Fern green   Black

Sepia Jade green Soft blue

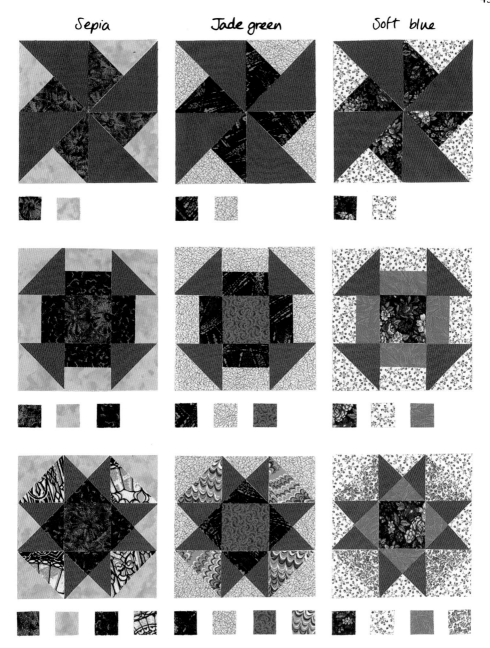

WORKING WITH PASTELS

PASTELS ARE THE pale tints of the color wheel: ice blue, soft pink, pale yellow, mint green, lavender, and apricot. These soft colors work well in modern home interiors, and their popularity has been enhanced, especially among first-time quiltmakers, by the trend for pastel bedrooms. Although pastel colors are very pleasing, they can be insipid unless combined with a stronger element. This can be provided by using some darker shades, or by introducing accents of contrasting color. If you want an entirely pastel look, use a distinctive design with firm lines to inject the required strength. Pastels can also be used in place of neutrals to soften the appearance of a strongly colored quilt.

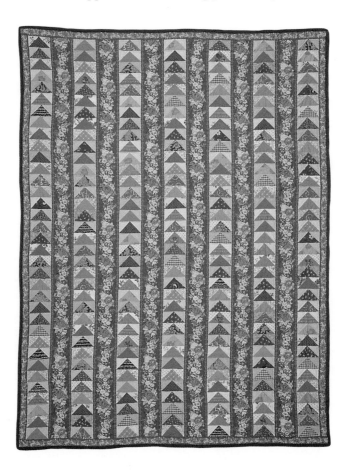

◄ NANCY BRELAND
"Flying Geese"
68 x 90 inches
This scrap quilt makes use of a collection of pale blues, pinks, and greens. The scraps were carefully selected to reflect the colors in the printed fabric used between the rows of geese. The strength in this soft pastel quilt comes from its distinctive traditional design.

▲ MARJOLŸN THOMAS
"Pastel Sampler"
26 x 34 inches
A variety of blocks are displayed in this attractive sampler quilt. The colors in the floral sashing are echoed by the light prints used to make up the blocks. These pastels are contrasted with darker shades of purple and green used throughout to give depth to the design.

Violet – 136

Barley sugar	Buttermilk	Clover pink

Slate gray   Bright turquoise   Bright red

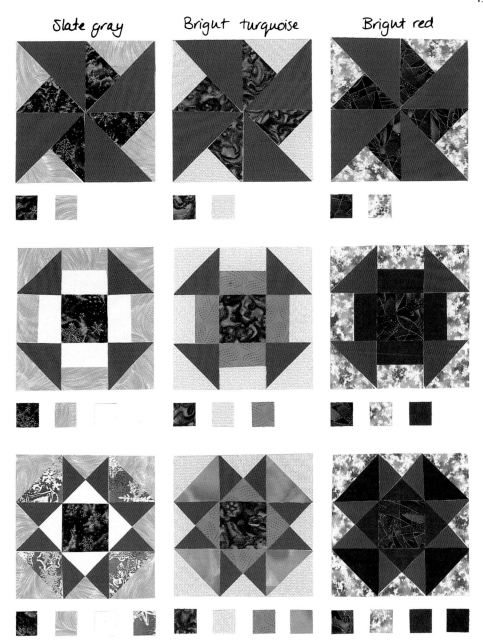

Purple – 52

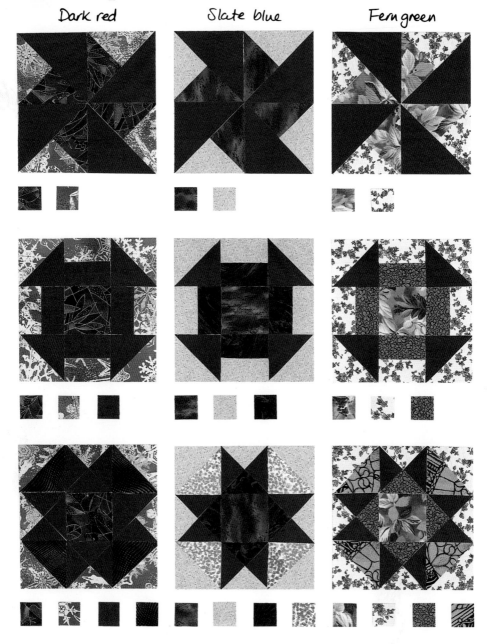

Dark red   Slate blue   Fern green

Marigold   Deep turquoise   Pink

Sand – 13

Bright turquoise   **Mocha**   **Forest green**

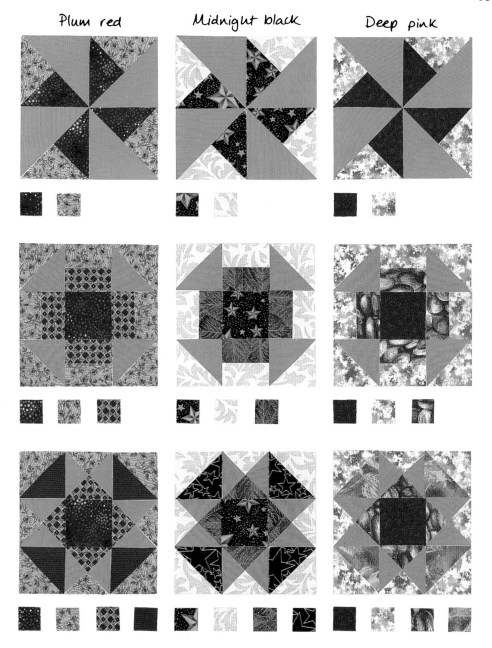

Plum red   Midnight black   Deep pink

Terra cotta – 46

Fern green   Burnished gold   Barley

Lilac   Peach   Jade green

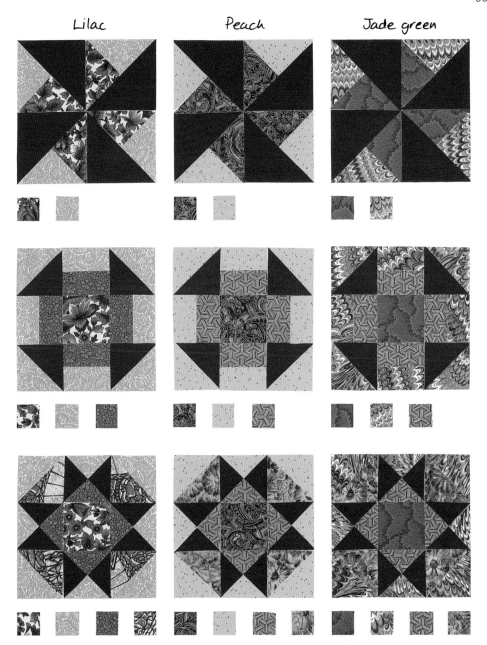

Brown – 06

Bright turquoise   Salmon pink   Imperial purple

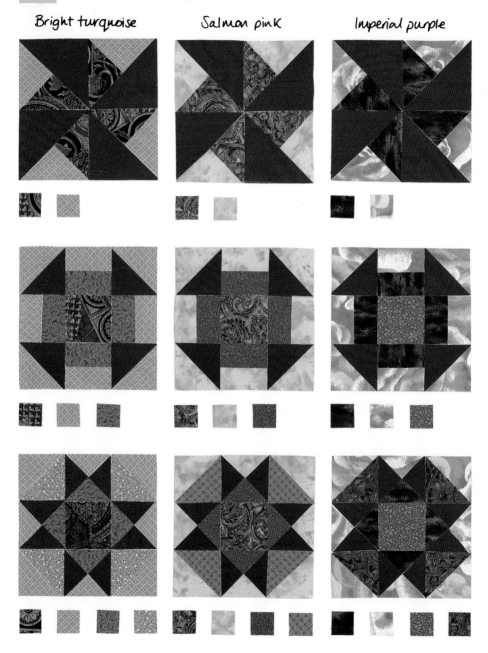

Leaf green   Bronze   Warm yellow

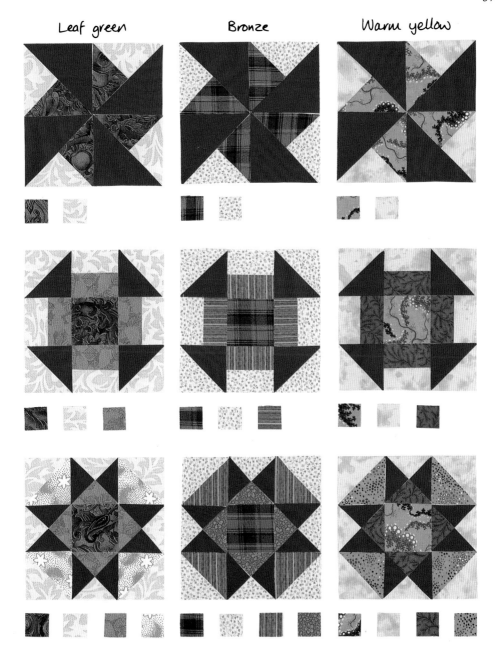

MONOCHROMATICS

"MONOCHROMATIC" CONJURES UP visions of black, gray, and white. Working solely with these neutrals is more difficult than it first appears, and strong contrasts are needed for a successful design. Touches of a color, such as red or gold, can be added for dramatic effect. The term monochromatic more accurately refers to combining fabrics in tints, shades, and tones of the same color, and these are some of the easiest schemes to put together. However, they can appear dull unless an effort is made to select fabrics which differ in value and scale. Including some neutrals is a useful way to provide variety without changing the character of a monochromatic color scheme.

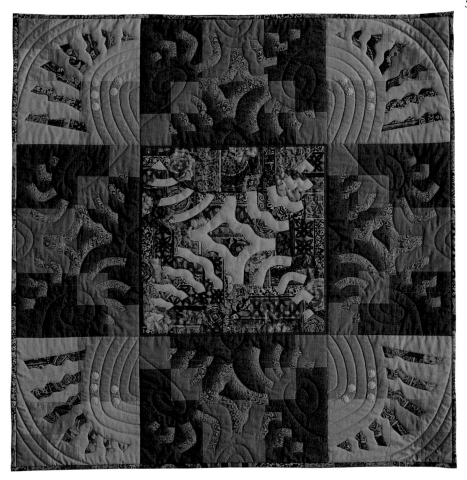

◄ ANNE WALKER
"Spinning Star"
36 x 36 inches
A quilt which uses only neutrals. The marked contrasts in tone and scale of the fabrics strengthen the design. The white triangles in the center of the star and on the bottom border add an accent in the same way as the introduction of strong color would.

▲ ANNE-MARIE STEWART
"Reverberations – Blue"
38 x 38 inches
Shades and tones of blue are effectively combined in this quilt. The contrasts in the value and scale of the fabrics used add interest to the design. The print fabric used as background in the central block injects a dramatic accent of red, which is echoed in the framing of the block.

Gray – 91

Eggplant   Ocher   Dark mauve

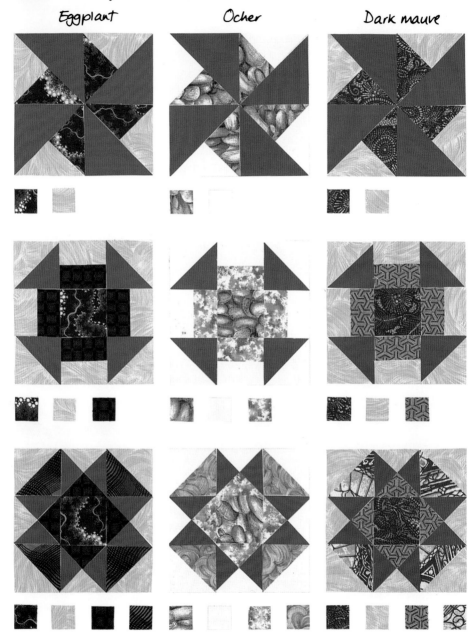

Periwinkle blue   Soft pink   Scarlet + black

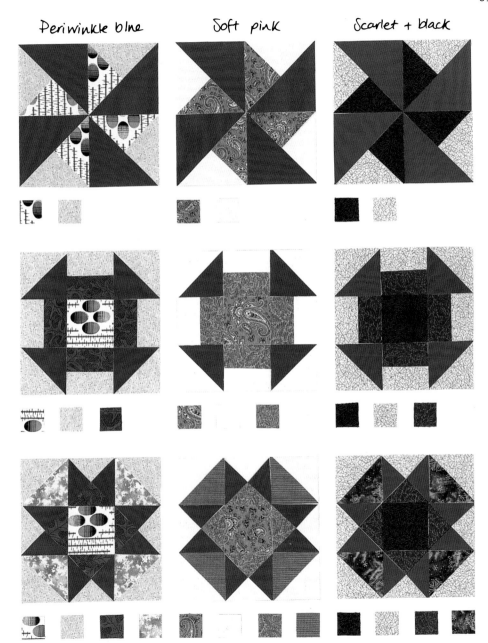

Black – K

Imperial purple   Black + white   Jade green

Forest green   Marigold   Bright red

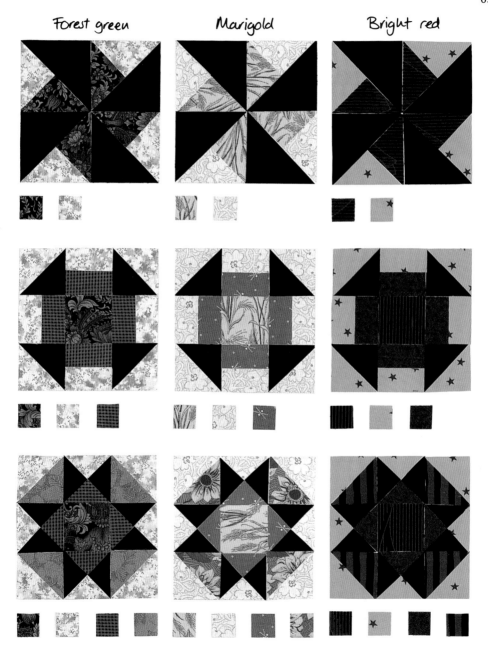

CREDITS

CONTRIBUTING QUILTMAKERS
18 Gill Turley; 19 Irene Kahmann; 29 Rosemary Russell;
36 Louise Mabbs; 37 Judith Gait; 46 Nancy Breland;
47 Marjolÿn Thomas; 58 Anne Walker; 59 Anne-Marie Stewart

Editor
Sally Butler

Art Editor
Clare Baggaley

Art Director
Moira Clinch

Editorial Director
Sophie Collins

Typeset in Great Britain by Poole Typesetting (Wessex) Ltd, Bournemouth
Manufactured by Bright Arts (Singapore) Pte. Ltd.
Printed by Star Standard Industries (Pte) Ltd., Singapore

The publishers would like to thank P & B Textiles for their generosity in
supplying the solid fabrics for the color charts